red silk sl

poems by

Marilyn Francis

Circaidy Gregory Press

red silk slippers

poems by
Marilyn Francis

Copyright Information

Printed in the UK
by MPG Books Group

ISBN 978-1-906451-13-4

Published by Circaidy Gregory Press
Creative Media Centre,
45 Robertson St, Hastings,
Sussex TN34 1HL

www.circaidygregory.co.uk
Independent Books for Independent Readers

For my father

About the Author

Living and working outside Bath in the defunct North Somerset coalfield, Marilyn Francis has mostly been a writer of things about British cinema (unpublished) and disgusted-of-Tunbridge-Wells letters to the Guardian Saturday Review and The London Review of Books. However, since completing a couple of Open University writing courses, she's taken to writing poems and short stories, some of which have been published in Earlyworks Press anthologies. Her story, 'Three Variations on the Enigma of Freedom' was recently published by RightEyedDeer, and her poem 'Work in Progress' was shortlisted for the Plough Poetry prize in 2008.

She is currently working on some ideas for a spoof sleuthing story set in an out of season seaside resort.

Cover Art

by Paul Francis

www.snappart.co.uk

contents

red silk slippers

Yesterday we celebrated all the Christmases
we'd missed since you left and this morning there's sunshine
and a light frost and I have red silk slippers from Thailand.

Outside, blackbirds peck for worms
on the square of turf where the old cat is buried
and I have bright wooden birds from Singapore to dangle
lifelike from the bare branches of the lilac tree.

The heating pipes grumble, wind lullabies
through the chimney and I have a lucky Chinese cat
whose silvered paw waves back and forth
tick-tocking the seconds
between yesterday and tomorrow.

This morning there's sunshine and a light frost
and I have red silk slippers from Thailand.

Birthday Present

For his birthday
she bought him a kite
shaped like a bird
and taught him how to fly.

They watched it wheel across the sky
hovering on the wind
dipping and diving.

A wild hawk began to fly with the kite.
They wove delicate patterns in space
in an airy *pas de deux.*

He took to a diet of raw beefsteak,
wore a black balaclava,
spent days in a darkened room.

She left.

He bought new lines for the kite,
flew it with the hawk
until they were both sky scraping specks.
They climbed too high in an electrical storm.

She picked up the singed feathers and string
packed them in a Tesco bag
along with his empty shoes.

Looking-glass

For seven years
it lay untouched
furred in dust
behind the water tank
where the spiders squatted

until at last,
swallowing a mouthful of fear,
she wavered a hand into darkness;
jerked the rosewood box
from its hidey-hole; tipped
a finger-shredding jigsaw
across the floor

piece by piece
she reassembled the daggers of glass

     threads of light filtered in
between the roof tiles
     though the filigree frame
        of a cheval mirror
where her reflection had once been

and when it was complete
she looked into the surface
and saw, in every frozen facet,
a miniature of herself.

Sometimes on Monday Mornings

I'd look through the curtains
that once had daisies on them
see the greying day
the globs of rain
easing down
through the window-crust,
and turn over, close my eyes
wouldn't open them again
until it was too late for work.

Only when it was safe
would I skive out
over the mirrored pavements,
dodging and weaving
through midday shoppers,
office girls out to lunch
and serious umbrellas,
to the Royal Manchester Institution
that civic, ionic temple to art.

I'd revolve through the doors
into the hushed brightness,
hear the solemn echoes
slow-march
along unseen gallery floors
and the muffled tip-tap of shoes
on the stone imperial staircase.

And from the gallery wall
Madox Brown's buccaneering shovellers,
muscular and headscarfed against
the heat of a Hampstead noon,
would eye me silently
chiding my indolence.

I'd stay until closing
mooching and watching
the light fade over the damp streets.
Idling away the workaday.

Mrs de Chirico goes shopping – a song of love

In the endless afternoons Mrs de Chirico goes shopping.
She knows the deserted arcades full of shadow and sun
the empty streets, the darkness crusted in eyeless archways,
the train caught on the horizon, black against the baby blue sky.

She thinks that today she will shop at the Greek's,
she loves his profile and his sad, sweet smile.
She buys two artichokes, ripe bananas, red rubber gloves,
a green ball, pomegranates and a fish.

Much later, with a shopper's uncertainty, she steps out,
into the stark chiaroscuro of the street. In the half-light
of home George has fashioned a mask
and nailed it to the living-room wall.

Lovelorn, he waits to hear her footsteps draw near,
a claw-hammer loosely held in his hand. A green ball
lies in a pool of bright blood, and up on the wall pinned
next to the mask is a limp, left-handed red rubber glove.

6

After the lights went out

we hunted blind
finger-tipping through sawdust and silverfish
to the back of the kitchen cupboard
groping for candle stubs and torches
the saved matchbooks
old newspapers and bits of wood.

We kindled a fire in the rusted grate
breathed a blaze to the god of the dark

and shadows danced
on the walls
to the half-forgotten songs of our clan.

We said silent prayers to the National Grid
to keep faith with the return of the light

powerless
as cave-dwellers
scared of the night
we waited for morning
to come.

Then somewhere a TV screen flickered
house lights blinked on
we were back in control by the flip of a switch
the night terrors had packed up and gone;
we made toast, brewed strong tea
watched *Match of the Day* on the box.

Dressing Table

wicker figure in a bonnet with basket of flowers
small framed print of daffodils

You were lost
at the top of the stairs
and asked for directions.
Your map-reading, you said,
had never been good.
Smiling politely you asked our names
and whether we had travelled far.

Kleen-e-ze hairbrush
Rimmel 60- second nail varnish [813 Euphoria]

We had the party without you that year
and though you beamed at the sight of a cake ablaze
with eighty pin-pricks of pink fairy lights
you were alarmed by the houseful of strangers.

cellophane bag containing two brass-effect buttons
brown glass bottle labelled glycerine and rosewater

You wore the greasy paisley apron
over your best white cardigan
and Sunday skirt. Someone had moved
the cooker and hidden the vegetable knife.
The saucepans were in the wrong place.

fumovate ointment
knitted viscose primary dressing

A confusion of bramble crept
around the kitchen window
scraping the panes with black thorns
tapping witchy-fingered on the glass.

reel of EFGEECO fishing line
plastic Quality Street tub containing 80 used candles

Sea-weed memories taunted you
played hide-and-seek. Refused to be netted
drifted away. Out of sight. You slept
for years on the narrow couch
while a tangle of briars grew in your head
until at last a princely kiss released you.

the eight of swords

another shagged-out afternoon
treading the path between
the municipal daffs spindling
in the sour grass
and the whoosh
of tea-time traffic
winding up to the top of the hill
like the Grand Old Duke
or Jack and Jill

in a snow globe of time
cups and coins
swords and pentacles
flurry through the air
lost and blind
I grab and catch
the eight of swords

'it's only a pack of cards'
says Alice.

Killing Time

Marooned in the endless summer
afternoon of my seventh year
scuffing the red Clarks sandals idly
at the curb-stone
willing something
to happen
I checked my tick-tock Timex watch –
time had stopped.
Dead.

Yesterday I checked the deathclock
it said I will die in my
seventy seventh year
I had only 642,686,343
seconds left
to kill.

Maybe I'll make a model
of the Eiffel Tower
in Swan Vestas.

Nocturne in St James' Park

I remember the park
darkening softly
in the closeness
of an early autumn evening
I remember us
secret in the gathering dusk
equipped for stealthy celebration.

I remember warm champagne
carefully carried
in a supermarket bag
I remember the taste
metallic fizz
tepid on the tongue –
the conjured clink of cardboard cups.

We didn't see her
pass through Queen Anne's Gate
cross Birdcage Walk
to the Blue Bridge
didn't hear her slip-slop feet
in broken shoes
heels askew
arms crammed with paper bags
of broken bread.

The sky filled with
razor silhouettes
the lake fizzed into life.
We saw her then
standing
arms raised
on the bridge
orchestrating
the night music.

I remember the sound
slicing
like a wire
through the dark.

Cat in the Grass

Here's to you
old cat in the grass
one-time terror
of the bat-squeak night
battle-scarred campaigner
of the dustbin wars
sublime songster
of the caterwauling dark.

Sprawled in a patch of sunlight
blackbirds bounce
a whisker-twitch
from where you lie
but I can see a glint
in that half-closed eye.

ghosts

a soft black fungus is climbing
up the twin towers of polystyrene coffee mugs from Denny's

and the Christmas cactus in the cracked ash tray
is covered in papery flowers

the Government Issue clock stopped at a quarter to five –
it's been afternoon for thirty years

soon the home-going workers will funnel into Russell Square tube
where there are no escalators and the lifts are kaput

they swarm down the one-hundred-and-seventy-five stairs
fanned by a hot desert breeze

the seventh day of the seventh month almost forgotten
in the crush and shove and 'mind the gap'

the platform so crowded you couldn't put an *Evening Standard*
between the tangle of bodies

going home to Winchmore Hill and Welwyn Garden City
passing the no-man's-land on Harry Beck's map

where the ghosts still wait at the platform's edge
though there hasn't been a train since 1932

Pegwell Bay

in the fag-end
of the out-of-season
season

you tread
the coast path
in serious boots

I am on the shoreline
swallowed up
by sky and clouds

I leave no footprints

Mona Lisa

Last year I saw *Mona Lisa*, she just
smiled from behind her bullet-proof glass
her eyes slanted my way, I'd say that she'd sussed
that it wasn't a joke, more like a farce
the sly way her lips curled had me nonplussed
I thought she must have a pain in her arse
Monsieur Duchamp clearly thought it was true
since he called his version L.H.O.O.Q.

The Jarrow Crusade

Marching south
to a harmonica band
to a kettledrum's beat
to the clip of four hundred newly shod feet
wearing Sunday-best suits and respectable caps
swinging arms to a kettledrum beat.
Marching south.

Marching south.
A fine wire of anger
a steely cold fire
twists
through the core of each man
marching south.

Marching south
down the country
 to Chester le Street
 Ferryhill
  Darlington
  Northallerton
  Ripon
   Harrogate
   Leeds
    Wakefield
    Barnsley
     Sheffield
     Chesterfield
     Mansfield
      Nottingham
      Loughborough
      Leicester
       Market Harborough
       Northampton
       Bedford
       Luton
        St Albans
        Edmonton

marching south so the world shall know of Jarrow
marching south to ask for work
marching south for our hungry families

                    to Westminster

to the House of Commons
to ask Mr Baldwin for work
                    but he was 'too busy to see us'.

Secret Windings

Asleep.
Eyelids closed,
soft as soot-fall
on secret White Rabbit dreams,
I follow a timeless spiral.
Look. No hands.
Watch me fall.
Watch me fly
headlong into darkness

on a never-ending staircase
the *Nu Descendant* clicks into
clockwork shards of motion
in a perpetual state of becoming
a cobra slowly uncoils
in a charmed
circle of
sound
reality is unwinding
unravelling
it dissolves
turning
in a sickening vortex
down, down
to the Davy Jones
deeps
of
the
night.

Mole

Mole, the poet, delves
into the earthy deeps
of the word-hoard,
nose and paws smeared
in choice phrases.

Head-full of rhymes
and rhythms he swims
clumsily to the surface
to await some Rattish distraction.

Pig Philosophy

The educated and enlightened classes
spend their evenings at dinner parties,
where they enjoy much talk and chatter
about the things that really matter.

Of Posh and Becks and Man United,
of all the wrongs that should be righted,
what was said and done, to whom, and when
will we ever see their like again.

After sage discourse through onion soup,
the conversation in unseasoned loop,
might shift to themes rich and diverse –
such as philosophy or rhymes in Erse

while those of us who know a thing or two
and are quite unmoved by onion stew,
would naturally prefer to get our fill
gorging on the works of John Stuart Mill,

and chewing the fat about this and that,
the pleasures of eating and having a chat –
would the happiness of the greatest number
be enhanced by a pickled cucumber?

And, what was Bentham's favourite jam?
Could the pleasure principle extend to spam?
Can a bean and sausage casserole
provide real nourishment for the soul?

But (surely you must agree)
this appetite for repartee,
is a perfect example (it seems to me)
of a pig-philosophy.

The Persistence of Memory

Caught in a camembert dream
I watched
as time draped heavy on a bough
slowly melted
and stopped
in a dark landscape
trapped
on the edge of delirium
along the bruised shoreline
a top-hatted surgeon
scalpel in hand
slyly advanced
on a beached umbrella
and a sewing machine.

Becalmed in a nightmare
a fly is caught in the drip of a clock.

On Fear of Poetical Analysis, or Terror of Dactyls

If the words don't reach
The end of the page,
And the lines
Form clusters or patterns.
You will guess what you see
Might be
POETRY.

If, when confronted with Keats'
'Belle Dame sans Merci'
You are unable to understand
One word in three.
You will know what you see
Must be
POETRY.

If Don Juan's ottava rima
Strikes cold fear in your heart.
Its failure to light up a fever
Needn't set you apart
From Byron's poetical art.
Though it might be the right lever
To move you. And fire you to see
The wit of POETRY.

So don't be alarmed by mere metrical feet.
A dactyl though dreadful
Is doubly unstressful;
Its metre elegiac and epic.
And if rhyme, rhythm, and metre
Won't inspire you.
And iambics and trochees
Have you beat.
Read Ginsburg and Kerouac
Get on the road and Howl... and, you will, undoubtedly, see that
stream of consciousness, continuous flow of sense perceptions,
thoughts, feelings and memories might still be POETRY

Christmas Shopping By Post

Three raw-faced farmers in a row
fancy-dressed in DJs and scarlet bow ties
drenched in disco beat, lip-reading
like the girls from Eagle mill –
and you in the chiaroscuro fug
sipping bubbles from a flute.

You did the shopping by post that year.
Essentials really, you said –
half of the Twelve Days sent to yourself

hibiscus flowers in syrup
Browne's chocolate marshmallows
Calabria baked fig roll
Australian celebration cake
black truffle chocolates
stem ginger in chocolate

not quite a Fortnum's hamper
but tasteful. An exquisite distillation,
a refinement in six arcane delights.

You'd sat at the bar of the Dorchester
in nineteen-sixty-five
drinking pink gin until it was time
for oysters at Quaglino's
and supper at L'Etoile
then racketing round to Ronnie's
to catch the cool   blue   vibes
and a late taxi to the Chelsea flat
in the twittering morning light.

Now, as the bitter minutes of another old year
thump towards *Auld Lang Syne*, and the moon-faced farmers
and alcopopped girls stomp it out to *Band of Gold*,
you drain your glass and leave, walking out past the fields
of rime-frosted sheep in your four inch Jimmy Choos.

Sisters

Side by side in Utility chic, they are doing the samba
down Luxborough Street.

Bums stuck out, bellies sucked in
doing the samba down Luxborough Street.

They are strutting their stuff, having a fling
stomping the pavement down Luxborough Street.

Amami perms, watermelon grins
they are watching the birdie on Luxborough Street.

Side by side in old ladies' frocks,
Brillo hair on seashell skulls.

Two old birds in owlish specs
peep from the depths of the floral chintz.

Still. Smiling for the camera.
Looking out the window to Luxborough Street.

A Villanelle On the Sad Demise of a Hoverfly In Reg's Caff

Pity the poor hoverfly
so brief to live, so soon to die.
It has no place to call its own.

Colourful as a circus clown
a stripy bumble in the sky
pity the poor hoverfly.

It buzzes round all passersby
heedless of each fretful frown
It has no place to call its own.

Though very pretty to the eye
who can stand the constant drone?
So brief to live, so soon to die.

And so we ask each other why
this irksome thing is free to roam
Pity the poor hoverfly.

Amazed, we watch as from on High
he is pulped by a rolled-up *Sun*
so brief to live, so soon to die
pity the poor hoverfly.

Waiting for the Person From Porlock

Waking early
to catch the night visions
in my spiral notebook
I gazed sleep-silted
at the pink-washed sky.
All words lost.

Then I saw it
flecked in dust motes
Earl Grey days done
though still a ladylike piece
brittle as old bones
redolent of tea-on-the-lawn
and the drowsy clip of croquet.

It was *A present from* the pleasure dome
a mimsy memento
chosen from the ranks of pot-pourri
and gingham skirted pots of jam –
a Crabtree & Evelyn hallucination.

Now, glaze cracked and handle gone
it bristles with blunt pencils –
reproaching me
as I wait at the window
for the person from Porlock.

Fell Walking

It was just getting dark, a drizzle-in-the-air afternoon.
Maybe it started out as a bit of a lark
a youthful remembrance
of roly-polying down sunlit grassy banks.
Did you helter-skelter over the edge all whee-ha
and wind-slice in the ears, buffet in the guts and plummet
through the air to a fairground sound in your head?
Did you take a chance against the odds, testing the gods,
nose-thumbing at age and the 'final shame of prudent
                                            commonsense'?

Later, when the final curtain parted
and the bits of you - the black fedora
the tarnished salpinx - all coasted through
and Bix played like bullets shot from a bell
when the ugly lumps of grief hiccupped
from some nameless place inside, I knew
that you were only taking the piss.

Oxymoronic

I can still see you
waving goodbye from the train
plastic flowers held tight in your fist
the dull shine of your damp moon-face
as you tried to smile –
a bittersweet smile.

I waited on the platform
as your train dissolved
in a gleam of cold fire
and a deafening silence filled the space
that once was filled by you.

Then I walked away –
crossed into darkness visible
with never a backwards glance.

The Machine Aesthetic
a house is a machine for living in – Le Corbusier

She was on early shift that week –
out of bed forty minutes after sunrise
gasping for a cuppa and a fag.

Lit the stove with a Swan Vesta –
eighteen floors collapsed
beneath her Marks & Sparks slippers.

It can be dangerous
to live in a machine –
whatever Monsieur Le Corbusier said.

This one had rolled off the assembly line
in concrete slabs and blocks –
assembled like a giant Meccano set

two-hundred feet in the air. It crumpled
like a house of cards when
Ivy turned on the gas.

Alice B Toklas Has Second Thoughts

I

Gertrude never had a second
thought she second guessed
the tick-Toklas seconds
ticked and tocked
the tick-Toklas seconds
tocked and ticked
the Toklas seconds
ticking and tocking
tocking and ticking
tick tock tick tock tick tock tick tock tick tock tick tock
tick tock
tick tock
never second best or second hand Rose

II

is a rose is a rose is a rose is a rose is a rose is a rose
Gertrude knows that Gertrude
is not second best
not best second
not second rate
not rated second
never second-in-command
commanding never second
it was second nature

III

thoughts are thoughts are thoughts
are not second thoughts not second
thoughts are thoughts once and first
first and once once and first
never twice twice never
always Gertrude thinks
to infinity

IV

infinity not second thoughts
Gertrude never had second thoughts
her thoughts are boundless
as yellow jelly seas
second thoughts never

The Last Fairy In The Pack

Wednesdays was always Brownies.
We met at the Church Hall glade
where half-dozens of Sprites
Elves, Pixies and Fairies
would learn the lore of the land.

We promised to be good
whenever we could.
Saved the Queen
and tied fisherman's knots.
It was all jolly fun
'good turns' were done,
we made tea, tidied up
and darned socks.
Badges were there for conspicuous flair
some had armfuls (sadly I'd none).

And at the end of the night
an arcane Brownie rite
would seal the close of the day.
In circles of sixes, Sprites
Fairies and Pixies
danced hand-in-hand
singing their own special song.

As Wednesdays piled up my anxiety grew.
What if one day there was only one-sixth of a six?
What if that sixth of the Fairies was me?
In solo circuit I'd have to sing out,
cheeks red and burning, inwardly squirming
tongue-twisted, face-gurning,
that awful milk-soppy song

we're the Fairies glad and gay
helping others every day

Now an Elf or a Gnome, a Pixie or Sprite
at least have a bit of street-cred
but a *FAIRY*.......?

Soon Wednesdays was TV instead.

Coming Down Sir John's Hill

In October
we counted the different kinds of rain
mizzle, drizzle, shower, cloudburst and squall
we watched the oystercatcher in the mist
and the 'heron priested' shore
from the rain smeared windows
of the poet's boathouse. Looking
where the tidal muds
curdled the Estuary waters.

Fleeing pots of tea and welshcakes
out
into a shower of bird-screech
climbing
Sir John's Hill for the view

halfway up
in the squelch and dread
of a rodeo-ed gateway
cows big as wardrobes
dared us to cross.

Bravado gone we shambled
mud-spluttered
shame-faced
back to the town.

Blackbird

Surprised by sunshine after days of rain
a mob of blackbirds swamp the garden
strutting their stuff like Saturday night.
Feathers ruffled and fluffed, they pogo
heads-up, heads-down, all along
the brim of the breeze-block wall.

Shamelessly randy they flirt too close,
careless of me and next door's cat
who eyes the gig from the orchestra stalls.
With a hip and studied cool she thinks
one might make a dainty dish,
a suppertime treat
for the queen of the garden jungle.

Belly to ground she creeps slo-mo
towards a succulent love-struck bird.

I pounce
grab the stalking fleabag
by the scruff.
Dangling at arms length
she spits
and swears she'll slice my face.
I drop her over the wall,
she'll dine on Whiskas tonight.

Unrequited: The Love Song of a 5B

Travelling via Borrowdale
and Derwentwater
latent with the power of words
and cross-hatched sketches
I'm smooth, stylish
elegant and thin
a Keswick Five Star
waiting now, sharp and trim
among chewed-up stubs.

Within my wooden shell
are endless graphite dreams.
I yearn for paper
of virgin white
as I wait upstanding
among my fellows
eager to pleasure the page
with artful arabesques.

This is my life

I don't go out
I don't need to travel
it's all here in my head
I can tell you all the capitals
of all the countries in the world,
all the names of all the players
in the 1952 FA Cup.
I can tell you everything about
the *solanum tuberosum*
except why anyone would
want to *think* about a potato.

I think a lot
some days my head
is filled with shadows
like November nights
seen through fogged-up
chip shop windows.

I'm working on a novel
it's all here.
I don't write it down
I don't like people
who write things down
I don't like people who write
me down.
Who write me
in black and white.

cold comfort

those gloves I gave you
that glittering Christmas
were finest kidskin

I bought them on a whim
in the spendthrift days
before the grey set in

you said you loved them
but you put them away
in the blue box
for best

you said they were
too good to wear
too beautiful for everyday

Peter Likes To Laugh

Peter likes fun.
He hoots like a train
laughs like a drain
a pun is too sly

for Peter. He is brimful
of chuckles, stuffed with guffaws
a barrelling bellyful
of hilarious applause.

He's a merry-go-round bellow
that eclipses the sun,
a roller-coasting holler.
An explosion of fun.

Helter-skelters of laughter
spiral up from his toes
a headlong pell-mell
just waiting to blow.

The roundabout echoes
ring in the air. You might say
he's a man who hasn't a care.
Peter is all the fun of the fair.

Evening In Paris

Stalled in film noir
a man waits alone
in a column of light

ghostly spirals of Gauloises
and cheap perfume
coil in the night air.

He waits.

Watches the street lamps stringing
out along the deserted boulevard.

Brassai, night wanderer
snapper of mist and rain,
the 'eye' of Paris, watches.
Waits in the dark to catch the street circus
as it creeps out of oiled rainbow gutters
seeps out of the monochrome dusk.

He is stopped at the edge of time
the final frame
a man alone in the fog.

Waiting.

Bananarama

We all know it
that old banana skin gag
that celluloid melodrama
from those slapstick days
before Cinerama.

A pin-striped man in a bowler hat
and a cane (it was always so)
puffed with conceit, striding
a city street (it was always so).
Slips, arse over tip, on a banana skin
carelessly dropped by a cute urchin.
Upended. All dignity gone.

Did we really roll in the aisles
splitting our sides
slapping our thighs?
Were our ribs so tickled
at the sight of a man oblivious
to rotten tomatoes and slippery peels,
of the need to avoid Life's custard pies?

Maybe in the fug of the dream-house
the world could be turned upside down
and maybe for just an hour or two
the victim's not you –
it's somebody else.

Guerrilla Gardening

It's gardening day in Parliament Square
Critical Mass and the WOMBLES are there
planting a shrubbery of grass and weed
in the People's garden at Parliament Square.

In the Worker's garden at Parliament Square
the ghosts of the Diggers and Winstanley are there
silently cheering the proletarian cause.
It's gardening day in Parliament Square.

Jack-the-lad, nimble Jack
blazing from a thicket of green fire
scales the monument
bloodied with paint
fast as a flame
quick as a flash
crowns
the dead statesman
in a stylish
Mohican
of turf.

It's gardening day in Parliament Square
red flags and banners are blossoming there
the red and the green in sweet harmony
in the People's garden at Parliament Square

In the Worker's garden at Parliament Square
Jack-in-the-green is burning there
a May Day pyre to welcome the Spring.
It's gardening day in Parliament Square.

Pinethwaite

The sky was overcast all morning
so we kept the lights on inside
the borrowed cottage. Outside
on the grass the picnic table
had turned turtle; its upside-down legs
frilled with raindrops.

Sodden with ennui, we watched
and waited for a change in the weather.
Nothing broke the shrouding weight of grey
until somewhere down in the woods
we heard the sharp clip of a hammer
and saw the sky gradually lighten.

The brochure promised us roe deer, squirrels
badgers and sixty-five varieties of birdlife,
but the solitary robin, who had scrutinised our arrival
with such beady interest, hadn't been back
and we'd had no visits from the representatives
of the remaining sixty-four.

Patches of blue elbowed through the cloud;
we switched off the electric light. Water
dripped from the plastic garden furniture
in languorous green globs. There was a knocking
at the backdoor. A duck with a twisted beak
had come to call. It was wiping its feet on the mat.

Protect and Survive

The delivery men took off its legs
to get it through the door
granny said it was as big as a Morrison shelter.

She crouched beneath it all that day
purling and plaining khaki socks
only stopping for a mouthful of Woolton Pie
and a slice of sugarless sponge cake.

We perched at its pristine edges,
like Alice willing the caterpillar to speak,
and nibbled on mushroom omelettes
as we waited for the table to shrink
to the optimum size
for a nuclear family.

We've had our fallings out
but time has absorbed the heat and the blast
and our words are scorched deep
beneath scratched crosshatchings –
all those love letters fixed in tears
and red wine.

Days are shorter now
and I know that tomorrow
the table will be as big as a Morrison shelter.

Rain Dance

Somewhere in the Mojave Desert
the ghosts circle. They leap
and stamp, left foot, right foot

circle-leap-left-foot-right-foot-leap-circle

It was the driest year since seventeen seventy two
and the Mother Red Cap ran out of beer

parched party-goers drank white spirit cocktails
on the pavement outside Camden Town tube
and each night they danced the sun up
and each day the temperature soared

a man fried an egg in the road
somewhere off Oxford Street
the swimming pools were empty
all the parks had burnt brown.

A Minister for Drought was chosen
not for his dancing skills, but somehow
three weeks later rain clouds began to build.

In the Mojave Desert
the ghosts are still dancing, circling
they leap and stamp, but there's been no rain

circle-leap-left-foot-right-foot-leap-circle

The Water Witch's New Year Revel – with eggshell coda

Samhain
when the roundabout seasons pause
midway between equinox and solstice,
and autumn gives way to darker beginnings.
Watch then, hidden by the water's edge
as the old year ends
and the water witch casts her boat
out onto the velvet waves.
Her broomstick paddle makes no sound.

Not one sailor will return tonight.

She greets the homecoming ships
with a whirlwind
calls up a tempest,
from the calm black sky.
In the eye of the storm
she treads a hornpipe
to a tune that's in her head.
The sea is a bubbling cauldron
of splintered wrecks.

No one will return tonight.

To save a sailor, like your granny said
on finishing your breakfast egg
turn the whole shell upside-down
smash it all to smithereens
for fear the witch might make a boat.
'For at old year's end, away from home
by night and sea, the witch will roam'.

Happily Ever After

Once
upon a time
weaving dreams
into her wedding shroud
she sang from the topmost turret
'a Prince has leapfrogged into my heart'.

Once
upon a time
she danced hand-in-hand
toe-tapping through the greenwood
chasing the snow-white bird in flight
to the confectioner's enchanted cottage.

Once
upon a time
spindle-pricked blood drowsily
trickled through a hundred unsullied winters.
Hedged and tangled by bramble and briar
she slept on until awakened by a Princely kiss.

Once
upon a time
free, she returned her lover
to his lily pad,
let her hair down, danced to a different tune,
paid her own piper; sang loud and long.

Work In Progress

Before *Janet and John* I read the cumbersome
books of upholstery samples whose soft pages
took both hands to turn and feel the textures
the roughs and smooths, the brocades, chintzes
the cut and uncut moquettes.

My father spoke through metalled teeth
cache of tin-tacks beneath his tongue
stub of pencil behind his ear.
Supine beside a beached and gutted settee
tip-tapping strips of webbing
Brylcreemed hair flopping
over the lenses of his National Health specs.

He worked somewhere behind Marylebone Station,
a lock-up that stank of mildew and sweat
where fibres floated in low-watt light.
He wore a chair-surgeon's apron, bibbed and cross-tied,
multi-pocketed, bristling with bradawls and bodkins;
needles like pirate's swords, scissors with crocodile teeth.

In time, the revamped ottomans, the Louis Quinze,
the button-backed, bow-legged chairs,
the Chesterfield in blue cretonne,
were restored to the drawing rooms of NW8
where my mother wiped wine rings
off marquetry tables
brushed fag ash
off Persian rugs
dusted the porcelain figures.
Walked the peke in the private Square gardens.

Circaidy Gregory

Independent Books for Independent Readers

Circaidy Gregory is a small press set up by Kay Green, writer, editor, and administrator of the Earlyworks Press Writers and Reviewers Club. Whilst Earlyworks Press exists to offer resources and good company to writers developing their careers, Circaidy Gregory is dedicated to the production of high quality, single author collections by writers we feel are going to appear in mainstream catalogues before too long.

Circaidy Gregory has so far produced first collections by three authors we have met through Earlyworks Press competitions and club activities. They are 'Light in the Shade' – short stories by Pam Eaves, who came to our attention after being shortlisted several times in Earlyworks Press fiction competitions; 'wormwood, earth and honey' – poems by Catherine Edmunds who was shortlisted in the Earlyworks Press High Fantasy Challenge, sci-fi and poetry competitions; and Kay Green's own 'Jung's People' which was originally published by Andrew Hook's award-winning Elastic Press. Also on our lists is 'Charity's Child' – an unputdownable novel by Rosalie Warren, who was shortlisted in the Science Fiction Challenge and whose story 'Touching the Rabbit' caused a stir in the 'Gender Genre' Challenge last year. 'Charity's Child' has proved a great success with library reading groups and Rosalie has since gone on to secure a contract with a larger publisher.

The book you are now holding is the first by Marilyn Francis, a poet we met through club activities and who has also been shortlisted in several competitions. 'red silk slippers' is the latest addition to what we hope will be a growing list of poetry that is fresh, accessible and intelligent.

Circaidy Gregory Press offers rewarding, unusual finds to readers who have high standards and enjoy searching out something just that little bit different.

To find out more about our authors, and our plans for the future, please visit our website – www.circaidygregory.co.uk

Kay Green February 2009